Ramblings of a Pagan Heart

Stories and Reflections from
"A Pagan Heart in Maine"
Podcast

By Robert "Greywolf" Webber Chipman

Pagan Heart Productions
Portland, Maine

To Sandy and Alta

Who have accepted all the crazy
and weird
that is me for all this time.

Contents:

"…AND WELCOME BACK TO A PAGAN HEART IN MAINE …"

I started a podcast in 2007 … I had a microphone and a computer and a voice … it seems that is all you need to make a podcast …

Each of us has stories and thoughts, and I wanted to share some of mine with others and it became a part of the podcast …

What we have in life is this moment, the past is past, the future is not here… yet what we are in this moment is born from our past… it's important to look back and, not live in the past or let it stop us from going forward, but take from our past the lessons that help us go forward…

I believe that by sharing those moments and the stories that each of us have, it makes our world larger, more connected…

Here are some of the stories of my life that I have shared …

I hope you enjoy them …

TURN LEFT …

I work in a 4-foot by 6-foot office.

My office weighs 36 thousand pounds and is made out of steel and fiberglass …

and rolls down the road …

I drive a 2020 twin screw Freightliner Cascadia and box trailer…

And I like driving …

Watching the open road …

Looking at the changing scenery around me…

I can read a map and find places…

I have driven my rig on city roads that even a car should never be on …

And never had a worry about it …

I am a professional and I am good at what I do …

And yet …

I have a problem …

The problem is that once in a while I have to turn on the GPS …

"*… ***Turn Left Now***…*"

I do not like my GPS …

It is not my friend …

And it all started with one word …

"*…***RECALCULATING*** …*"

It is that word that digs at my very heart…

Recalculating…

I am a professional driver and I have driven and logged over 2 million miles of our nations great highways…

So when I hear my GPS say…

"* …***Recalculating*** …*"

What I hear is…

"* ***Great job Copernicus!!… missed a turn again*** !! *

I hate my GPS …

"* …***Turn left … Your other left …***

Idiot … Recalculating … *"

I swear at my GPS…

I use language that used to get my mouth washed out with soap when I was a kid…

" …__Oh for the love of god … Do I need to get out of this box and drive myself … Recalculating__…*"*

I call it a LOT of bad names ...

"…__Hey Stevie Wonder…That was your turn back there… Recalculating__…*"*

Sometimes I feel it doesn't give me enough time to turn…

"…__turn riiiiiiight … NOW !!! Recalculating__…*"*

Sometimes it will lead me to Gods' forsaken backwoods places where they may have filmed the movie "Deliverance" …

"… __turn right … I hope you like banjos__…*"*

I swear this thing is possessed…

It will be only a matter of time before it starts dripping blood and quoting passages from some dark eldritch text …

"…__Iä! Iä! Cthulhu fhtagn!__…*"*

So here is the thing …

I know that my GPS is not out to get me …

it is just doing its job and helping me get to where I'm going …

I know that when my GPS says …

"*… <u>Recalculating</u>…*"

It isn't doing it to me personally...

I like to think I'm in control of my driving and where I need to go ….

After all I am a professional and I don't like being told what to do … so when it says …

"*…<u>Recalculating</u> …*"

It is easy to feel like I did something wrong and I'm being judged for it…

Life can be the same way…

I like to feel I'm in control of everything and when I'm not, I feel sometimes like the universe is out to get me…

That perception is not true…

In life there are accidents up ahead...

There is construction. There is traffic…

Sometimes we move too fast to make the right turns…

Sometimes people will cut you off…

Sometimes you find yourself in neighborhoods where you don't have the faintest idea where you are…

That's why sometimes it is good to find your own spiritual, Universal GPS…

Everything has reason…

Everything has purpose…

Sometimes you just have to ask the universe for directions…

Find out where you are and where you want to go, then listen to what the universe tells you…

It will help you get where you are going.

It is easy - for me at least - to think that the whole world is out to get me at times…

That for some reason the Universe is making things harder than it needs to be.

I DO believe that there is a reason for everything that happens. So when things don't seem right and you are a little lost, it is good to listen to your Universal GPS when it says turn around, turn left, turn right …

Do some recalculating, because at some point you're going to hear the universe say…

"* ***…You have reached your destination. Welcome…*** *"

I AM A PAGAN …

I am a Pagan and a Witch, and I want to go ahead and define that a little more because there are a lot of misconceptions about what those two words mean.

We'll start with what I mean when I say I'm a Pagan.

I believe in individual spirituality, and what I mean by that is each of us has an individual personal relationship with Deity.

If I gave everyone in the world a pencil and paper and I asked them to draw a picture of God, (assuming everyone had the same talent for drawing) every picture would be different. Why? Because every person has a different, personal relationship with Deity.

As an example, when you look at your father you see him a certain way, as your father. Whereas your uncle would see your father in a totally different way, as his brother.

We each see God differently. We may see Deity as god, goddess, father-son-spirit, mother, daughter, sister, teacher, mentor, friend.

When we give deity a name we are calling out and acknowledging the aspects of Deity that goes with that name.

There is a running gag that if you ask ten different Pagans what Paganism is you will get twelve different answers, and I'm not going to set in stone a definition of Paganism or Spirituality. I want to share and celebrate the sheer diversity of spirituality as a whole.

I do not believe in blind faith, so when I share my thoughts and my path you may say to me "Why, THAT is exactly what I believe!" and that is great if you do.

You also may instead say "Greywolf, I don't believe that at all and I think your nose looks funny when you say that!" … And that's great, too!

At least you know what you believe, or at the very least, you know what you don't believe.

I am not a Christian yet I believe in God. I am not a Wiccan yet I believe in the Goddess. The dual nature of Deity is the source of life itself and is evidenced all around us.

I believe in the balances and lessons found in the natural world and that my personal relationship with Deity is found in Nature …

I believe that our true knowledge and the lessons we are to learn in our life do not come just from books but from living life itself and from the connections we make with those around us.

There are universal truths to be found in all faiths and cultures and just like there are different flavors of cakes out there, they all start with some basic ingredients ... flour, water, salt, and sugar.

Ingredients like Love, Compassion, Joy.

These ingredients are found in all paths, and it is when you embrace the common ingredients you find Peace and connection to Deity.

SPUNKY HUGS…

I was sleeping nice and peaceful one night when suddenly I had the feeling that I was pinned under a burning couch.

I woke up to find that the "burning couch" I was pinned under was actually a twenty pound cat sitting on my chest. His little cat face was gazing into my eyes from about one inch away.

I calmly said, "Spunky, it's 3 o'clock in the freaking morning, you need to get down now."

Then I gently pushed him off of me and onto my wife Sandy.

I rolled over, thinking we were done here, and tried to go back to sleep.

I say "tried" because I felt and heard this loud commotion behind me and my wife saying "It's three o'clock in the freaking morning, go away!" to a twenty pound cat sitting on her chest.

I was going to point out to my wife that Spunky already knows what time it is because I had just told him when he was sitting on MY chest.

Then I thought that might be a bad idea since that would take all the attention away from the cat and put it all on me.

That would have brought up a whole bunch of sentences like, "How did the cat get off of your chest and onto MINE!" and "He's YOUR cat, DO something!"

So long story short, I had a cat sitting on my chest again.

I pushed him off and he came back.

"Fine," I said, "just lay there and go to sleep."

Oh, but it's not that easy. The cat decided I'm not "fluffy" enough for him to lay on.

He decided he needed to "soften" me.

Spunky does this in two ways.

First he stands up, and then places his feet very carefully, one each, on my spleen, liver, kidney, and bladder.

Then he shifts all of his weight onto each of his paws in order, so that it feels like someone is driving a mop handle into my gut.

That was still not good enough. He proceeded to fluff me like a pillow.

It wouldn't be so bad, except that attached to the end of his paws are these little razor blades he calls claws.

It was three o'clock in the morning and I was being slashed to pieces like a teenager in a horror movie.

Fortunately our cat has a mental defect, other than the fact he likes to have attention paid to him at 3 o'clock in the freaking morning.

His defect is that he hates to be held. He likes attention, but the minute you put your arms around him his eyes get really big and round, his fur goes POOF and zoom, he's gone.

So I gave him what we call in our household, a "Spunky Hug." I put my arms around him, his eyes got big, his fur went POOF and zoom, he was gone.

I smiled, and I went back to sleep.

My questions to you are:

"What is the burning couch in your life that you are pinned under?"

"What is the twenty pound cat sitting on your chest?"

"What is keeping you from sleeping at night?"

"Do you push it off, Does it keep coming back?"

"Do you shift it onto someone else? Family, friends?"

Whatever you push off, chances are it will keep coming back, and eventually will start slicing you up.

So try this, give it a "Spunky Hug." OWN it. Pay attention to it. Find out what mental defect it has that will make it go away.

I know it sounds easy. Sometimes it is.

Sometimes it takes work.

Don't just ignore it.

Give it MORE than the attention it wants.

Take the problem and give it a big hug…

Because if you just push it off, it is just going to make the ones you love mad at you and it will end up coming back anyway.

BALLOOVALUTIONISM …

My college years were short but created many interesting memories.

One of those memories was around midterms my first year.

I remember spending a lot of late nights studying, eating a lot of ramen noodles, and drinking a lot of 3 liter bottles of cheap no-name soda.

It was one of these nights, sitting with my roommates studying, that my brain was about fried.

I needed to do something totally different from studying so I said to myself, "Hey, why don't I start a cult?"

I have a bit of a warped sense of humor.

So I want to introduce you to the cult of BALLOOVALUTIONISM!

Now stay with me on this, we are going for a little trip.

Balloovalutionism is the belief that our species evolved from balloons.

We are evolved balloons.

I'll let that sink in for a moment.

Some of the ideas I had was that the universe didn't start with the "Big Bang," it started with a Big Pop."

When the balloon at the center of the universe popped, all of matter was created by the broken pieces of latex scattered across the void, or what I refer to as the "Balloonaverse."

Each of us carries traits of our balloon ancestors.

From the moment of conception a woman's womb grows, much like a balloon.

During labor we tell her to breath, to blow, "huff, huff, huff." This is to finish blowing the child up before birth.

When a child is born it is connected to the mother by the umbilical cord, or what balloovalutionists call … its "string."

When the string is cut the baby is a free balloon! It takes its first breath and inflates. Some babies are born all wrinkly, too little air, and some are born chubby, too much air.

As the child grows it regulates its air by breathing, without air the balloon dies.

All the organs in our bodies are there to help keep our skin, our "living latex," flexible.

We are constantly emitting air from one end or another to regulate our internal pressure.

As we grow older our "skin" isn't as flexible and we get smaller and wrinkled, just as a balloon does when it gets old.

Some people believe that we evolved from balloon animals, but they're a bunch of clowns.

There are many balloovalutionists, or "Loons" for short.

Some Loons have fully embraced Balloovalutionism and have become enlightened "Balloonatics" joining the "Order of the Mylar" to spread the word of Balloovalutionism everywhere.

And the how do balloovalutionists worship?

It is very simple. Balloovalutionists remember and celebrate our balloon evolution and each year on their birthday, or "ballooning" day.

They surround themselves with colorful balloons, surround themselves with friends and family and share a cake.

That's it…

That is all it takes to become a Balloovalutionist. Many people are practicing Balloovalutionists and don't even realize it.

And THAT is how you start a cult.

So here is the part that is scary, I have shared this idea with many friends.

Most "sane" people would look at me and say "Bob, you're scaring me, stop it."

Yet, most of the time what I hear is, "You know something? THAT kind of makes sense in a weird sort of way."

(Quiet chanting in the background "One…Of…Us…One…Of…Us.")

So I share this story to share this observation:

There are people in the world who would look at my "balloon cult" and say, "Ok, you're insane, I'm out!"

Then there are the people who "get it," who understand that this was a thought exercise and would embrace it because they understand the meaning behind it.

Then there are those who are desperately searching for answers and grasp onto anything that has a ring of believability. People who want to belong to something larger than themselves.

THAT is why people embrace cults. THAT is why people will sell all their possessions and give all their money to TV evangelists, or follow someone who "sounds" right.

Many people want to "belong." They want "answers" to all their problems. They want someone to tell them how to live and that they are on the "right" path.

This is why I believe it is so important to question EVERYTHING.

Blind faith in what people say or what people write has a glaring problem.

It's blind.

It is far better to ask the questions, study more than one point of view, and have an educated, clear and open faith.

This applies to everything, not just religion.

This is YOUR life and it's good to be able to see where you are going.

I AM A WITCH …

What I mean by that is I believe in natural energies around and in us, that ALL of us use from time to time that help shape our lives.

Have you ever thought about a person and that person calls a few minutes later? Or known who is on the other line before picking the phone up?

Have you ever taken a side street for no reason and found out you avoided an accident by doing so?

Do things happen to you, that seem like coincidences but perhaps happen too regularly?

All people have intuitive abilities and use them whether they realize it or not.

Witchcraft in its basic form is being aware that there are energies around us and using those energies for a purposeful intent. Everyone has this ability.

I look at it like breathing. Everyone breathes but you are not always aware of it because you do it all the time. and usually the only time you become aware of it is when you stop breathing.

Witchcraft is like breathing with a purpose. Let's say that purpose is to blow out a candle. First you become aware of your breathing. You take a breath in. You direct your breath toward the candle and let your breath out and the candle goes out.

That is Magick. That is Witchcraft.

Energy is all around and in us, just like air and taking a breath. It is about Awareness, Intent, Direction, and Release. That is basic Magick.

TEACUP…

Have you ever noticed that when someone is confused or trying to understand what you are saying that sometimes their head tilts to the side?

There is a reason for this.

The brain is like a teacup. It only holds a certain amount of information before it starts to spill over.

So what people do is if their brain starts to get full they have to dump out some of their thoughts to understand what you are trying to tell them.

So they tilt their head

I find a lot of people tilt their head when I talk.

This is not necessarily a good thing because I realize they may be dumping out really good information they have learned over the years just to try to understand my ramblings.

My nieces and nephews learned this at a young age. They would ask me questions. I would answer them. Their little heads would tilt to the side and valuable knowledge would be lost forever.

"Why is the sky blue?" they would ask.

"Because it's not green," I would say, "if it was green you wouldn't see the outlines of the trees."

"Oh…" and their heads would fall over to the side.

"How does the grass grow?" they would ask.

"The gophers and chipmunks push it up from underneath?" I would say.

"Oh…" heads slowly tilting to the side.

Eventually they learned an important lesson, and that is to never ask Uncle Greywolf any questions because Uncle Greywolf is crazier than a loon.

But children are like that. They are very quick to dump good information for whatever new thing comes along because they are learning and trying to figure out what is good information and what is bad. I'm always amazed at what is kept as good information.

When my niece was five she was playing in the house one day. One of our cats walked across the room and I was bored.

I said to my niece, "That's a 'snicklefritz' kitty".

She looked at me and said "No, that's Fluffy."

I said "No, her NAME is Fluffy, but she is a 'snicklefritz' kitty."

Her tiny little teacup of a head tilted to the side and dumped out everything her five years had taught her about cats to listen to what I had to say.

"The way you can tell if a cat is a snicklefritz is if you listen to them really hard they will make a sound like 'flibbertigibbet.'"

Her eyes lit up and she made a beeline for the cat.

Entertainment comes in many forms. For me that day it came in the form of a little child chasing, catching and holding a cat up to her ears like a boom box waiting for it to make a weird sound.

Fluffy was not happy, and the cat had to put up with days of this knowing that it couldn't scratch the "human kitten."

I guess the moral of this is just that the next time you are listening to someone and you find yourself tilting

your head, make sure you're not dumping out something
important you may need later

OH, WHAT A WORLD! WHAT A WORLD! …

I think its important to also share what being a Pagan and a Witch is NOT …

1) - We do not fly around on broomsticks. Why? Because there are no seats on broomsticks. I'm a rather large person and even if I was sitting sidesaddle, it would be very uncomfortable. If I have to fly I'll take a plane, and even then I'd rather walk.

2) - We do not kidnap and eat children, not since that whole Hansen and Gretel debacle.

I mean seriously … here is a nice old witch minding her own business in her home made of candy. Suddenly these two city kids get themselves lost and start chowing down on the shingles on her house. So what does she do? She knows they are lost, so she invites them in and offers to feed them until their parents come to pick them up… and THEN the kids try to push her in the oven!

It's always the same story. "Burn the witch! Burn the witch!" When the cops show up the kids tell the authorities that the witch was going to EAT them.

So you can see, it is just not worth the trouble.

3) - We do not turn people into frogs. If I could turn people into frogs, can you imagine how many frogs would be in the world today?

What do you say to an angry witch?

… "Ribbit." …

4) - Do we wear black cloaks and pointy hats?

… Sometimes… I LIKE pointy hats! …

Yet most of us wear normal everyday clothes. Do people dress up for church? Yes of course ... and so do we.

5) - Do we dance around nude in fields and in front of bonfires?

OK, You got me there, but let me just say, unless you have stood out in a field naked in a summer rain don't knock it.

Of course, if you live in a suburb or city you might want to avoid running around in your birthday suit. People might get the wrong idea.

You don't have to dance naked to be a pagan, but why not?

I personally do not dance naked unless I am alone. A three hundred and fifty pound, pasty white fat man, prancing and frolicking naked in a field like some demented wood pixie tends to create a disturbing image for many people.

I do try to follow a "harm none" rule.

6) - We do not throw people into volcanoes.

It's very hard to find a volcano here in Maine, and volcanoes seem to get very hot when you get close to them.

Hollywood has painted a picture with lots of special effects and stereotypes of what they think a witch is and is not. Sadly, ignorance and fear has added the rest.

There are many people who have mistaken definitions of what Paganism and Witchcraft really is about based on movies and what non-Pagans and witches "think" it means. Do you want to know what we are about?

Ask.

We do not proselytize or try to convert people, but if you are interested and ask us questions about paganism we would be more than happy to talk with you.

So unless you find yourself talking to little cartoon birds sitting on your shoulder, you do not have to worry about biting into that apple the old witch gave you.

I AM A NERD …

I think I was about 8 or 9 years old when I got my first pair of glasses.

Back then there was no real choice of frames. You had your basic 1970's dark brown or blue plastic rims with large lens.

From the first time I put them on and I looked in the mirror I could see clearly that I was a nerd.

I didn't plan on being a nerd, it just seemed to fit. I enjoyed reading lots of books. I enjoyed science. I actively tried to avoid any sporting activity. These are just a few of the signs of a traditional nerd.

I learned at an early age that sports equal pain.

My memories flash back to grade school gym classes and being required to play "Dodge Ball."

The coaches had always called dodge ball a "game," yet I always looked at it as a Darwinistic form of survivalism.

The rules were simple. Basically all of the weaker members of the tribe are herded to the center of the room while the stronger members circle them and proceed to pummel them to death with bowling balls coated in hard rubber.

These balls were called "4-square balls." I believed that they referred to the earlier form of nerdism, known in the Fifties and early Sixties as "squares," thus the balls were "for squares".

Nerds came in basically two flavors when I was growing up. You had your spindly tall variety and you had your short and round variety. I fell into the short and round classification.

When the Dodge Ball game started, all of the tall spindly nerds would hide behind the four foot round nerds standing in the center of the room in the hopes of surviving a few precious extra moments before meeting their dire fate.

I did not like gym classes.

I didn't like sports.

They hurt.

There was the saying "No Pain, No Gain"

MY saying was "no pain, no PAIN!

As I got older I wondered what it would be like to be a part of the socially "hip" crowd.

I have always considered myself a relatively intelligent person and yet this one area has always eluded me.

I was convinced that it was my glasses, that maybe if I had 20/20 vision, I would have been accepted as one of the "cool" people and welcomed with open arms.

So I grew older and I got contact lenses.

I promptly forgot about my old life as a nerdy caterpillar with glasses and was ready to embrace the life as a social butterfly.

You can imagine my surprise when this didn't happen.

I became a nerdy caterpillar with contact lenses.

It took me a long time and well into college before I realized that it was a different type of nearsightedness that made me what I was.

There are a lot of things I could have changed to make me part of the "popular" crowd, and as I grew I did try on different looks and different attitudes.

It wasn't me. I kept coming back to the things I liked… computers, science, reading, watching shows like "Doctor Who" and "Star Trek."

I came to the conclusion that rather than fit in with the "hip" crowd, that I should just fit in to who I am.

From that point I went from being a nerdy caterpillar to being a nerdy butterfly.

It was about making the changes in my life to be who I am, not to become someone I am not.

I am a nerd. I am a computer geek. I think the clarity of sight is in knowing and accepting who and what I am.

I wear glasses to help me see. It doesn't matter what other people think.

The other day I reached up to adjust my glasses, and promptly hit myself in the head for no reason.

I forgot I had on my contacts lenses, and I had forgotten because I am so used to wearing my glasses. They are a part of me.

Sometimes to see clearly all you need to do is give yourself a good poke in the head.

THE MAGPIE …

The magpie is a large bird that belongs to the same family as crows, ravens, and jays.

The black-billed magpie lives throughout Europe, Central Asia, parts of Siberia, and North America from Alaska to New Mexico.

The magpie is a common bird, seen in parks and suburban gardens.

They are scavengers and collect objects, with a weakness for shiny things. They are fond of bright shiny things that interest them as toys, play-pretties, or something to stash away. They like to hoard things.

I have come to the inescapable conclusion that I am a magpie.

I can't help it.

If I'm shopping and I see some small shiny trinket, my eyes get a shiny glaze to them and a smile will cross my lips.

The next thing I know I have a shopping cart full of small objects to take back to my nest.

It's an illness and it cannot be helped.

When I get home and my wife sees me bringing in bags of swag that wasn't on the grocery list she asks "What's this?"

"It's mine! It is small and bright and shiny and it will make a nice addition to our nest," and I smile.

I collect things.

I find that if I have one of something then everything is OK. The moment I have two of something it becomes a collection, and I must have more.

Currently I have over thirty Tarot decks in my collection and counting.

Why? because I had one Tarot deck and someone gave me a second Tarot deck.

It became a collection.

Like a packrat I cannot throw things away. I had a 10 foot by 20 foot storage unit that was filled to the rafters with objects collected for over 20 years.

A few years ago my wife asked me two questions.

The first question was, "Why don't we go through your storage unit and throw away all the junk?"

The second question was, "Why are you looking at me like that?"

That storage unit was a reflection of me. Like a time capsule or an archeological dig, you could go through the various layers and find chapters of my life.

Each object had a purpose. We started going through the storage and Sandy asked "Why do you have a broken table lamp?"

"Because I can fix it one day and we will have a perfectly good table lamp… you never know when we might need a perfectly good table lamp. ''

She looked at me sadly and said, "But we have table lamps at home… new ones… that work … not covered in dust."

Then she held up the lamp and my eyes glazed over and a smile crossed my lips.

It has taken almost 3 years, yet the storage unit is emptied. Some of the stuff went to second hand charities to help others, some things went to the dump.

Some things went to my workshop to be hidden away from a loving wife who has no idea what it is like to be a magpie.

It's an illness.

We hang onto a lot of things we don't need.

Sometimes it's good to go through all that stuff, things, ideas, and experiences we have collected over the years.

Get rid of the things you really don't need in your life. Keep the good stuff and get rid of all the junk. It's not easy and it could take years.

You will find that as you get rid of the broken stuff you have more room in your life for all the things that work.

THE BEAT OF THE DRUM …

Music is important, and we are musical creatures.

More than that, we ARE music, each of us, each of our lives are a song. YOU are a song and, follow me on this, we are instruments. Our life is learning to play the instruments that we are.

So how do you learn to play an instrument?

You practice, and you learn, and you practice more… and then when you get done practicing? You practice even more.

Life is the same way, we learn to play the same way, and the notes we play are the things we do in life.

I look at music simply as three parts:

The rhythm, the beat of the music.

The melody, the heart of the song.

The lyrics, the meaning of the music.

So let's look at the beat. What is your rhythm, what is your beat and how do you find it?

First you can find a basic beat right on your wrist.

Find your pulse.

Feel the thump-thump, thump- thump, thump-thump.

There is where you start.

You are alive.

You can find rhythm in the world.

You find it near the water, in the waves lapping the shore.

You find it in fields, watching the waves of the wind against the grain.

You can hear the rustle of the trees.

Find the patterns, go outside and really listen to the world.

In the city you can still find the rhythms.

I drive through many cities every week and I can feel and hear the rhythm of each, whether the sleeping rhythms of 3 am or the hectic rhythms of rush hour on the freeways.

Within the larger rhythms you find the smaller rhythms.

A dogs bark, an alarm going off, horns blaring.

Pigeons… by the Gods, pigeons everywhere.

Don't listen to the sound, listen to the rhythm. Find the ones that you like.

Don't listen to the blaring alarm, just listen to the rhythm of it.

Bump, bump, bump, bump, bump.

Don't listen to the dogs barking, but just the rhythm of the barking.

Bump, bumpbumpbump, bump. Bump bumpbumpbump, bump,

Find the rhythms that feel right, the sounds of the woods and the sounds of the city.

48

Each hold the rhythms of life, and just like finding and tuning a song you like on the radio, tune into the rhythms of the world around you and find the ones that resonate with your personal rhythm, your heartbeat drum.

You will learn to play with them when you start concentrating on the rhythms.

You WILL find that the patterns in your personal world will start balancing, and you may find rhythms in places you hadn't thought before.

GENIUS…

A while back my wife and I helped a friend put together some furniture.

Not real furniture, but what I call "bachelor" furniture. This is the furniture that looks like wood, but isn't. It is actually made out of 500 pounds of glue and sawdust.

In my youth I put together a fair number of these sawdust constructions and most of the time I don't even have to look at the instructions.

I put together his television stand like I was a professional. Of course I don't really know if that's a good thing or a bad thing.

Our friend told my wife that he thought I was a "genius" that I could put together these particle board cabinets so fast without even looking at the instructions.

Sandy told me this and so I said smugly, "Why yes, yes I am a genius, aren't I?"

I started to put together a fine, well-constructed sawdust desk, all the while glowing in the admiration of my wife, when suddenly we had a minor problem.

Part of the desk looked like the letter "H" and the dowels that held them together wouldn't go together. I banged on the side of the "H" and nothing happened, so I pressed on the sides. Still nothing.

So to get more leverage I leaned forward putting my head between the boards and pressed on the sides.

It worked!

The two boards slammed together… with my head squarely pressed in the middle like a particle board sandwich.

I very quickly let go and I fell backward and my glasses went flying. I ended up with sawdust scratches on my, now narrower, head.

My wife came running over and worriedly asked, "Are you ok?" while trying to stifle a thinly veiled giggle.

I look up at her and said "Why yes, because I'm a freaking genius."

All of us at times have momentary lapses of sanity and clarity.

Common sense tells most people to not to smash their face with particle board, yet sometimes people get so caught up with themselves and their self-importance that they forget the people and situations around them. The next thing you know… WHAM!!

DON'T let this happen to you. There is a big difference between intelligence and common sense.

You can have all of the schooling and degrees and papers hanging on your wall telling the world how smart you are, but if you don't have any common sense you might as well slam your head between a couple of boards.

At least people will laugh.

54

THE HEART OF THE SONG…

This is the melody, this is your song.

Your life is your personal melody. Each of us has a song we play. Some people play their song well and others have difficulty playing the notes.

Our song is our thoughts, our dreams, our decisions, and our choices that lead us there.

Our song plays to the end and it has many changes, many movements, happy notes and sad notes.

What song do you want to play?

We are always learning and practicing and sometimes we hit wrongs notes that don't sound right. We all make wrong decisions and bad choices at times. We all hit wrong notes as we are learning.

So don't play that note again. Keep learning, and then when you find notes in your life that sound good write them down and you will find your song.

You can find the notes for your song in your own head, in the decisions and dreams you have.

Take it one step at a time. If you are new at playing this instrument called life, then start with the basics.

Don't try to play a whole concert if this is the first time you've picked up an instrument.

To learn any instrument you first learn to play the basic notes and find the ones that sound right together.

You make basic chords, you take the first steps to get your song, your life, in order.

The key is that even if your song is simple at first, that you practice hitting the right notes, soon you develop what's called "muscle memory."

When you learn to type, you learn where the keys are, in music where the right notes are, where the right keys in your life are.

Practice, you will hit wrong notes and make wrong decisions. Even the best musicians have off days.

Keep practicing, and then start finding your inspiration.

Remember this is your song and it can be a simple jingle or a grand concert …and they are both wonderful… jingles are just as important as concerts.

I find the inspiration in my life from the world around me and, in this particular chapter in my life, from the quiet places rather than the noisy places.

As important to the notes you hear around you is the silence in between the notes.

If you know how to read music take a piece of clear plastic and make a musical staff on it.

The next time you look at a bunch of clouds in the sky take your plastic out and see if it forms a melody.

If you can't read music then play three notes in your head. A low, middle and high note, hold your plastic up to the clouds and look at the low, middle and high clouds and play them in your head. You may be amazed at what the universe is playing in silence.

56

Bottom line, take the time to look at the clouds.

Are they thick heavy metal clouds or are they soft rock clouds? Are they folksy clouds or disco clouds? Find the silence and fill it with quiet song.

When you go to make your day to day decisions, listen to the song you found. Look for the tunes playing in silence around you.

Be aware of what is playing and be aware of your song within your surroundings.

I drive down a lot of four lane highways and at the top of hills I can see several miles of song laid out in the cars ahead of me.

Each lane a line on a music sheet.

When you start finding the way you want your song to sound, start playing.

Start making the heavy metal, or the soft rock, or easy listening decisions that you want your life to be.

SPRING...

Our family is awakened from our winter hibernation to find it slowly becoming spring here in Maine.

The days are getting warmer and flowers are starting to pop up in the flower beds, and it is time for spring cleaning.

This is where I think there is a big difference between men and women.

Men don't see dirt the way women see dirt, and part of this is the way most are brought up, but I think a lot of it is just the difference between how men and women think in general.

Here is how it happens in our family.

We wake up from our winter hibernation, my lovely wife looks out and sees the snow melting and birds singing. The birds start to build their nests for spring, getting rid of the old straw and bringing in the new.

Sandy starts to get ideas and she smiles.

She starts looking at our nest, and with all the spring thinking and birds and nesting and such. It does something to her eyes. They become hyper focused... and they see dirt. Microscopic dirt covering everything.

Now don't get me wrong, we keep a very clean and nice house, and we pick up after ourselves and we dust, but this is "SPRING"... and the old straw has to go.

I, on the other hand, see spring a little differently. I look outside, and I see the snow melting, and then I see the dirt.

I start getting ideas and I smile.

I start planning my garden. I start to root around in the flower beds. I WANT to get dirty.

Men do not see dirt the way that women see dirt. As little kids, the boys would play in the dirt. We would crawl around in the dirt with our toy trucks, stomping in the mud. As we got older we would hike around the woods and large sand pits, ride our bikes down dirty trails. When we got scraped and cut we would rub dirt in the wounds to stop the bleeding.

Working in the gardens we would become part of the land. We were one with the dirt, and dirt was our friend.

So my love and I do not see dirt the same way.

She announces to our roommate Alta and I that, "It is Time!" and that "We can start by spring cleaning the living room."

I look at the living room and say in my naivety, "…but it's not dirty."

She looks at me as if I am insane, and then my sweetheart takes me by the hand as she would an idiot and points out that we need to wipe down the walls and ceiling, clean the windows and frames, and clean the carpets, pulling out all the furniture and wash the drapes …. because they are "dirty."

As the idiot male, I have no clue as to what she means because I cannot see dirt the way she does.

Dirt is my friend.

So I move all the furniture and steam clean the carpet. Alta cleans all the knickknacks and Sandy wipes down the windows.

After washing one window she says to me, "See the difference between the two windows? See how much cleaner one is compared to the other?"

Of course I look out the one window. I can see the yard and a few ducks in the yard.

I look out the other window. I see the yard, and a few ducks in the yard.

Me, being a guy, understands that there is really only one right answer to this test.

I say, "Oh Yes! Yes this one is much clearer!'

Sandy looks at me and says "It was the other one I cleaned." She shakes her head, turns and walks away.

Of course I can see dust and dirt. It just has to be a little bigger to be noticeable to me. I don't see dust until it becomes deep enough to plant seeds in.

We clean our nest and my sweetheart is happy to see all the little dirt go away, and I start my plans to play in the dirt outside.

It is Spring!

THE LYRICS TO LIFE…

Lyrics are words that are couched on the waves of the song. They can form messages or just accents.

Once you find your beat and start finding your melody, then you can share your message with others.

It can be a simple "I love you," or "I'm here for you."

It can be a call for others. "Where are you?" "Find me."

Words have meaning.

Words are powerful.

Your message is important and needs to be heard.

This is your song.

This is your life.

When three things, Your Beat, Your Melody, and your Lyrics, come together, you will start finding other members of your band.

You will find friends, family, people in your life that share the same rhythm and form the right chords in your life.

Use your voice, your lyrics to find the people in your life that add depth to your song.

You will also add depth to THEIR song.

They may be playing a different set of notes, yet that is how you make chords.

It is how you make music.

SNORKY SNOOTS…

Sandy and I went to get new tires for the car.

We sat in the waiting room watching TV and it had on a preschool children's program with some type of alien critters running around.

One looked like a pet octopus, and another looked like a dog with an elephant nose, and they were chasing this spaceship which just happened to be the size of a Frisbee.

I could have changed the channel to one of the news stations, but sometimes it's nice not to know too much of what is going on in the world.

As we watched these alien critters on TV, I said something about one of the alien pets and my wife asked "Which one? The octopus or the dog with the snorky snoot?" and I said, "The dog with the snorky snoot." And we continued to watch TV.

I started to process the conversation we just had and then my brain handed me a note and I smiled.

It was a smile of sudden realization that I may not be the craziest one in the room for a change.

I slowly turned to my beautiful wife with that smile and she got worried.

She knows me well enough to know when I'm grinning like an idiot then it is time to worry, and she said "What?"

I incredulously asked, "Snorky snoot?"

She said defiantly, "Yeah…snorky snoots. There used to be a cartoon called 'The Snorks' that lived under the sea and the had these 'snoots' coming out of their heads… snorky snoots."

I was amazed, not so much that my wife had come up with this word to describe something, but also that I had understood exactly what she had meant immediately.

Perhaps the word had existed all along and just needed someone to say it out loud. It wasn't planned. It just happened.

It gives me a warm feeling and a sense of security knowing that the people I love are as crazy as I am.

When my wife and I had been dating about a month we went driving up to my family's home in central Maine. We drove past some chickens by the side of the road.

Without thinking I said, "Oh look! Chickens! bok bok, bok, bok!"

There was a brief awkward silence.

I then said, "I said that out loud, didn't I?"

She said, "Yup."

Awkward silence.

With a heavy sigh, I said, "Well that's just great. Now you think I'm nuts. Here I am clucking at chickens walking on the side of the road … I mean sure, it's ok if you do that with cows. If you see cows in the middle of the field it is perfectly acceptable to roll down your window and do a drive-by 'mooing …'"

For about 15 minutes I talked about why it was ok to make cow noises at cows, but if you do that with any other animal it's just plain weird.

She laughed and laughed about that.

Seven months later I asked her to marry me and she said yes.

We talked about that day and she told me that while I was saying, "Oh look! Chickens! Bok, bok, bok!", SHE had been thinking the exact same thing, only she didn't say it out loud.

It was at that moment when she said she knew she had fallen in love with me.

There is warmth and security in knowing the people you love are as crazy as you are.

Each of us has an incredible gift, a spark of discovery, and of creation within the child nature we all possess.

I don't think many people realize how powerful that gift is. We can create things, we can create words and stories.

Here is the thought that really made me want to share this story. We spend a good part of our lives looking and searching for happiness and joy, but we don't have to look.

We can "create" happiness and joy!

The next time you drive by a cow roll down the window and go "Mooo!"

Make up words that mean something to you.

Take some paper and doodle.

Go buy some clay and make a little figure or a vase.

Let the child in you come out.

Don't just look for joy and happiness.

Create it!

GONE FISHING…

I remember the first time I went fishing as a kid. It was on the coast of West Haven, Connecticut, off of a little place called Savin Point. I had a small fishing pole and for bait we used little silver fish called shiners.

I learned how to cast and bait my own hook from my Dad and my older brothers.

We were there for a few hours and I hadn't caught anything and then WHAM! Something grabbed my hook!

I started reeling my line in and the fish did something I had never thought a fish could do.

The fish jumped out of the water… and it flew… like a bird… for about 30 feet before going back into the water.

I stopped reeling in for a minute, because even as a young kid I knew a thing about fish… mainly that they don't fly.

It seems I had caught an "Exocoetidae" or "Flying Fish" and that was how I was properly introduced to the time honored tradition of the fisherman.

I spent a lot of my spare time when I was young down on the beach and piers fishing, or on the river or ponds.

I hadn't found time to go fishing for quite a few years and said to Sandy, "I need to go fishing again. We live less than 100 yards from the ocean so I feel I should be out there dragging seafood onto the beach to feed our tribe. right?"

She surprised me this past year with two tickets for a chartered deep sea fishing trip.

Sandy and I got on the boat with about 15 other people and went out to the harbor to go fishing.

It was a beautiful day, sunny but not too hot, with light fluffy clouds drifting by. The fish must have known we were coming because they were nowhere to be found.

In fact, the only fish that was caught was a small mackerel by a teenager at the back of the boat.

We catch many things in life. We take our fishing rig, bait our hooks and set our lines. We go fishing for the things we want.

Sometimes you may catch something totally different and then you have to adjust and just go with it. Like a Flying Fish it could just be a fish that thinks it's a pelican.

You catch things for a reason, and sometimes it may feel you are trying to find something, to catch something and it seems you haven't caught anything.

It may be you did catch something, but you just didn't know it.

Sandy and I didn't catch any fish that day, and yet we spent a wonderful afternoon on the ocean, in a boat with a wonderful breeze, and as we headed back into shore we sat on the deck and watched a brilliant sunset while holding hands.

It was a perfect fishing trip.

ADVENTURES IN ROLLER SKATING…

The scene is a large roller skating rink. Carpet covered walls and half wall dividers surrounding a hardwood floor with disco lights.

Lots of people skating around in a circle. The time is 1980 and I am about to have my first whirlwind romance.

First, I should introduce you to the roller skating scene of the late 1970s and early 80s.

We didn't have inline skates or the heel skates that the kids are fond of today.

We had "real" roller skates. They were lace up boots with 4 wheels set at the corners so they looked like little cars.

The moment you strapped these contraptions to your feet, gravity was no longer your friend.

Learning to skate was a challenge.

I started with "The Spider Walk." This is where you cling to the wall like a spider slowly pulling yourself around the rink.

Once I mastered that I moved on to "The Frankenstein." This is where you hold your arms out in front of you and slowly clomp your feet trying to get your wheels rolling.

That leads into "The Zombie." This is where your arms are out in front of you and your legs are straight, but at least you are rolling.

Sometimes it is helpful to just have a friend push you around the rink.

After a LOT of practice things started to "click" and I was skating like an Olympic Champion.

Learning to stop is a whole different story.

There is the simple "Drop Dead" technique.

This is where you fall, plain and simple. You skate along and when you want to stop, you drop like a rock.

The people behind you however will not be impressed, and will show their displeasure by running into you at breakneck speed, the key word being "break neck".

Then you have the "Stripper Pole" technique.

This is when, as you are going around the rink, you reach out and grab hold of one of the poles supporting the ceiling, spinning you around the pole.

You have to hold onto this pole as if your very life depends on it …

It does.

There is the simple "Wall Splat" technique.

This is where you drive your body straight into the wall.

It helps to spread your legs and arms out as far as you can so that when the wall hits you it spreads the pain evenly.

A similar technique for stopping is the "Windshield Move."

This is where you aim for the wall that is half wall, half Plexiglas. This gives an incredible show to people on the other side of the glass as you hit the wall like a bug against the windshield of the car.

Then there is the "Olympic Dismount".

This is when you run yourself into one of the half walls. There is a bonus if you have built up a lot of speed for this one.

When you hit the half wall as fast as you can, your body is bent in half and you go flying head over heels onto the other side, saving you the trouble of actually leaving the rink of your own volition.

There is the "Unexpected Stop."

This is where you accidentally touch your skates together and they instantly stop, while the rest of your body makes a ninety degree turn straight into the hardwood floor.

The sound you make when this happens is "eeeerk, WHAP!" unless you are fat like me, in which case you bounce like a stone being skipped along a lake… "eeeerk, WHAP! … whap, whap, whap, whap!" until you hit a wall or another skater.

That brings me to a technique that I had almost perfected.

I call it the "Misery Loves Company" technique.

This simple move is when you reach out to one of your fellow skaters for help.

What I mean by that is that you reach out and cling to the nearest person like a drowning man to a piece of driftwood.

Usually what happens is that you end up taking him down and using the poor unfortunate "driftwood" as a cushion to keep you from going "eeeerk, WHAP! … whap, whap, whap, whap!"

This brings me to how I was introduced to my first brief encounter with true love.

Instead of really learning how to skate well, I learned how to skate fast.

It was while skating fast one day that I noticed this beautiful blonde girl crossing the rink to go get a soda. She was going fast at a perfect right angle to the direction I was going.

I made some quick calculations in my head and realized in a moment we were destined to meet and I knew it was true love when her eyes met mine and came to the same conclusion.

It's amazing how the realization of true love looks a lot like total panic and terror on a woman's face.

In a blur of high speed flailing, we met.

Our left arms hooked each other and we spun like the blades of a helicopter.

Our legs went straight out and our love lifted us completely off the ground and we landed…

"WHAP!… whap, whap, whap, whap!"

It was as if the whole world froze around us and we were the only two people in the world.

Some people may say it was the concussion, but I disagree.

Alas, our time together was short lived, for my heart was a sailing ship full of love, and her heart was an iceberg floating on the ocean of life.

She laughed, got up and disappeared into the crowd as my heart sank in those frigid waters, and the world came back into focus and people kept skating around me.

This is the world, and each of us are trying to keep our balance.

Each of us finds things to hang onto.

We learn to skate, and if we stop the world keeps going around us.

Sometimes people crash into us and we fall.

Sometimes we trip ourselves up.

Yet it is what we do after we fall that is important.

Get back up, smile, laugh, start skating again and then see what happens around the next corner.

THE BALANCE…

I look at balance as if I'm riding a unicycle and juggling at the same time.

Riding the unicycle is your everyday journey with all its bumps and challenges.

The objects you juggle are the different areas of your life… the physical, mental, spiritual and emotional.

The first thing I learned when riding a bike or unicycle is that it is easier to balance when you are moving.

If you try to balance on a bike that is standing still, it is a lot harder than when you are pedaling.

So keep pedaling.

If you just stop and let the world crash around you, it is very hard to look forward to really see where you are trying to get to.

Balance is not a destination, it is a state of being, and if you are on a unicycle you have to keep shifting and pedaling back and forth to stay upright.

Life is like that.

The world around us is constantly changing from moment to moment and it is important to keep aware of the conditions immediately around you so you can shift with those conditions that affect your life.

Keep moving.

The other part of the balance is juggling the different areas of our lives.

There is the Physical … work, exercise, eat, pay bills, keeping the car running, etc.

There is the Spiritual…the bigger picture we are all a part of, our connection to Deity, being "grounded" and staying connected.

There is the Emotional…being aware of our emotions, knowing where they come from, managing them.

There is the Mental… your own inner playground, the places in your head that you go to find things that interest you.

You can include any of your own descriptions into these areas and maybe your definitions would be completely different from mine.

There was a time when I believed that everything in the world was orderly and linear.

I would try to set up a nice stable list of priorities and expect that as long as I did letter "A," then letter "B" would come next, then letter "C."

I figured out that life wasn't that organized or simple.

I can honestly say that there were quite a few years that I had gotten the feeling that life really didn't like me.

It is important to have priorities, yet priorities can overlap and a lot of time they cannot be pigeonholed into just one place.

If you watch jugglers you see they have control of many objects in the air at one time.

Each object seems to overlap and become the next.

This is the same with the objects we juggle in everyday life.

Each area overlaps into another.

Our mental, spiritual, physical and emotion areas crisscross and take each other's place.

So how do you find balance?

It's in the secret of juggling.

No matter how many objects are in the air, there is only one or two in your hands at any one time.

The rest are in the air.

You make sure that the object you are holding is going to be tossed in such a way that you can catch it again when it comes back down.

It is magical and, in the hands of a juggler, objects dance and seem to move with a purpose all their own… all in balance.

So I juggle. I hold onto each area of my life for a moment and then set it free to soar up and then catch the next area for a moment.

It is not as hard as it looks, it just takes practice.

Lots and lots of practice.

Life is a ride. Keep riding and keep looking ahead.

Look at where you are going.

If you look down at your feet you can't see what's in front of you and you will fall.

If you look ahead, you can steer through most of the rough patches. Lean into the wind and don't let it blow you over.

What do you do if you do fall?

You get back up, take a breath, and start riding again.

Everyone juggles. You may not call it that, but everyone does.

The key is not to spend too much time with one thing in your hands won't be open to catch the next object.

Do not ignore an object and let it drop.

It is a dance.

Things get busy, and things get hectic but keep juggling.

You may have to adjust the pattern.

Toss a few objects higher to have time to catch the other objects.

This is where priorities come in.

Make lists … lots of them.

One of the keys to balancing is to see what you need to catch before it hits the ground and make allowances for that.

Find your priorities.

Learn how many things you can juggle.

If you try to juggle too much then everything falls to the ground.

It takes practice, but don't stop.

Keep moving forward.

CHINESE FOOD …

I love Chinese Food.

It's not that I "like" Chinese food.

I LOVE Chinese food.

Sometimes I have Chinese food 3-4 times a week.

I just love it. I drive between 300 and 500 miles several days a week all over new England and upstate New York, and usually I plan my trip so that it lands me by a Chinese restaurant or buffet.

Buffet is such a wonderful word. In some of the buffets you can find a "Mongolian Grill."

This little corner of heaven has a guy who will cook the food up in front of you and hand it back with a smile. First pick up a plate and head for the long counter with foods on it.

The first part of the counter has your "critters" on it. You've got your land critters, your sea critters and your critters with wings. You take a big scoop of critter and put it on your plate.

Then you go get some plants. There are all the basics. Chia sprouts and leaves and such and THEN you get to the "bonsai" food. Little, itty, bitty, ears of corn, about 1 –2 inches long.

I always imagined the little 12 inch stalks these ears of corn must grow on… little tiny fields of miniature corn.

Then you get to the noodles… angel hair noodles, rice noodles, egg noodles. You take a yourself a big, old, helping of that.

Then you add your spices and oils… garlic, ginger, spicy oil, white wine, and a whole variety of different sauces.

Once you have your plate full, then the magic begins. You hand the plate of food to the Mongolian chef and 3 minutes later he hands you a fully cooked meal.

The only time I have ever seen my wife jealous is when I'm flirting with the Mongolian chef.

I've mentioned to her that it wouldn't be hard to add a grill to the kitchen and I'm sure that the chef would love to live in our spare bedroom.

I find that I order almost the same things every time though.

I mean, I "look" at the whole menu, yet it always boils down to the favorites… Wonton soup, lo mien, sweet and sour chicken,, teriyaki… Every time.

We all like what we like, And that's not a bad thing.

I have no real point or message for this story, just that I like Chinese food.

Maybe THAT'S the message, that you don't have to have a point or message to the story.

I think I'm going to go order in some Chinese food.

THE SKUNK AND I …

As a teenager I would spend part of my summers on my grandparent's farm. The farm was about 3 miles from my closest friend's house and there were many nights that I would find myself walking home in the dark, down back country roads.

It would get really, REALLY dark and this was not a good thing as I had always been an avid fan of horror movies and books.

As a child I fed heavily on the works of Stephen King, H.P. Lovecraft, Arthur Machen and Edgar Allen Poe.

So, having a rather vivid, yet warped, imagination, you can see how a pudgy, 14 year old kid walking through the woods with only the moon shining down can lead to an overwhelming sense of dread and foreboding.

I never was afraid of the dark.

I was afraid of all the unseen horrors lurking "in" the dark.

I would come up with wonderful strategies to fend off these horrors. One of these strategies was singing and whistling and making sure that anything around me knew I was there. I didn't want to accidentally startle any unseen denizen of the terrible night.

This worked for a while until my imagination handed me a little message… and that message was that maybe the monsters are trying to find me and I might have well been shouting "Over here! Pudgy little kid waiting to be eaten! Come and get it!" … so the singing stopped… and the listening began…

With every little sound I expected some monstrosity, borne from the depths of unseen dimensions, to reach out its tentacles and drag me kicking and screaming into the forest never to be heard from again.

It was thoughts like these that made for an exciting and fascinating childhood.

One evening while walking home, and waiting for my eventual doom to present itself to me, I was heading up the quarter mile dirt road to my grandparent's place when I saw a small creature waddling down the road toward me.

I slowed down…

and it slowed down…

and then I saw the white stripe down its back.

All the imagined terrors quickly fled from my brain to be filled with the actual small terror in front of me.

The skunk started waddling right over to me and I froze in place in the off chance that maybe it would think I was just a really fat leafless tree.

The odiferous creature saw thru my ruse and promptly walked over to sniff my feet.

I had been walking for a couple miles and didn't know if it had smelled a kindred spirit emanating from my sneakers, but I remained frozen in place, thinking pleasant thoughts like "nice smelly kitty," and "No threat here."

The images of me being sprayed by a skunk and having to spend several days washing and living in the shed did not excite me in the least.

Then the true horror of my unfortunate situation presented itself in the form of 3 more small furry striped objects.

A Momma Skunk and her two babies were walking down the hill on the opposite side of the road!

In that instant it all became clear to me. It wasn't my feet papa skunk was interested in, it was making sure his family was safe, and the message was crystal clear.

I was staring down the barrel of a fully loaded skunk and if I made any sudden moves, BAM! I wouldn't have any close friends for a week.

Well, Momma and her babies continued down the hill and when they were far enough away, Papa Skunk looked up at me and said, "Good day, sir," and waddled off after them.

I waited there until I figured I was out of his shooting range and continued my walk toward home.

The monsters I had imagined didn't bother me as much any more.

It seems that sometimes we walk through a lot of dark places on our journey home…

And that it is easy to imagine all the horrible things that can go wrong in our day to day life.

When things are dark it is usually our own thoughts that terrify us more than what is actually out there.

Sometimes we are faced with situations that really stink, and yet most of the time, it is important to just take care of the problem at your feet.

EVERY DAY, A COW …

As a teenager I enjoyed playing the arcades.

My first job was delivering newspapers in the neighborhood and each week I would religiously take my earnings and spend them one quarter at a time in the arcade machines.

"Asteroids" and "Space Invaders" were a few of my favorites, but pinball was my true love.

I was playing a favorite Bally machine one day with my friends and was racking up a very high score when one of my friends bumped the pinball table and tilted my machine.

He said he was sorry but I didn't feel it was very sincere, especially since he was the person I was playing against.

I took my revenge and cursed him with a curse that, upon the very words, influences all who hear it.

Don't worry, it's a very simple and harmless curse.

So I wiggled my hands and fingers in what I assumed was a mystical fashion in front of him and with a solemn voice pointed and said, "Every day, a cow."

My friend said, "What?"

I said "Every day, a cow … It's a curse … What that means is that every day you will see a cow or something that will remind you of a cow, could be something as simple as a glass of milk, or a cow on TV … every day… for the rest of your life"

He laughed…

and my friends laughed…

and I laughed and laughed.

I like to think my laugh was more of a sinister, maniacal laugh.

I didn't see him for a few days but when I did he gave me a weird look.

He came over and said, "What did you do to me and how do you make it stop?"

I said, "huh?"

He said, "Cows .. all I've been seeing is cows, on the side of trucks, billboards, I'm seeing cows everywhere!"

Of course, I told him the bad news that the curse could not be broken, but it could be shared and by sharing it would slowly go away.

All I really did was make him aware that cows are around us every day, we just take it for granted.

We become disconnected from what is around us and we don't even realize it.

It's about being aware.

I talk about this a lot because many of the stories I share about my life are about things that have made me aware of my place in this world.

To be aware and awake to what is around you is one of the most important things in life.

I have not seen my high school friend in many, many years, and yet I still like to think, that every now and then, when he sees a cow, he remembers the curse and the times we had at the arcade.

SEND IN THE CLOWN …

Clowns are evil… they just are.

Ask any six year old child if a clown is evil. They will tell you they LOVE clowns!

They are ok when they are on TV or in a circus, but put a clown within arms reach of a six year old and watch. Children know the truth… and I know.

I used to be a clown.

When you are young, you sometimes have funny ideas of what constitutes a viable career option in today's world … for me, it was being a clown.

I said to myself, "How hard could it be? Do a little juggling, go a little overboard with the makeup, and then sit back and make millions of dollars as many clowns of the world have done in the past!"

What can I say? I was young.

What they don't tell you is just like the Jedi, there is a dark side.

I first came to realize this when I received a call from a young couple who wanted a birthday clown for their 5 year old daughter.

The call went like this.

(phone rings, I pick it up) "Hello?"

(Parent) "Yes hello, are you a birthday clown?"

(Me) "Why yes! Yes I am! Juggles the Clown, at your service!"

(Parent) "We would like to hire you for our 5 year old's birthday party!"

(Me) "Ok, I charge 50 dollars for a half hour or 80 dollars for an hour show …"

(Parent hesitantly) "There is only one thing… she is deathly afraid of clowns…"

(dramatic pause)

So basically what this parent wanted me to do is torture the child they loved and adored.

My thought was that for an extra 20 dollars I could bring a bloody axe to chase her around the house and they would get to keep the ax so that in several years when she has blocked out this disturbing episode from her life they could just leave it on her bed with a note saying, "I'll be back for this!! .. signed …The Clown!"

Back to the phone call…

(Me) " Sure, that shouldn't be a problem at all!"

The thought about the axe should have been a warning that I may have been leaning toward the evil side of clowning.

I showed up at their house and walked into the group of about 12 children.

I noticed the birthday girl immediately.

She was the one standing and staring at me with a look of frozen terror on her face.

The other children clapped and shouted for joy "The clown is here, The clown is here!" knowing that the clown had not come for them.

The birthday girl's eyes were wide as saucers and I saw what was reflected in those eyes when she looked at me.

She saw hair like the flames of Hell licking a bleached white skull!

Lips and chin stained red from the blood of its innocent victims!

Painted eyebrows raised high in judgment over all it surveyed!

All of this in the reflection of this innocent child's round, large, mirror-like pupils.

So for the next hour I entertained the kids while the birthday girl made sure to put other kids between me and her.

I could see the thoughts in her brain…

"Why did my parents do this to me!?"

"Here!…take Billy, Billy would love to be dragged to his doom!"

"How about little Suzy? I don't even like the little thumb sucker, my mom made me invite her!"

"Please take any and all of them, O Spawn of Satan! But spare me!"

It was a fun evening.

As I got ready to leave, the birthday girl slowly came over to me and held out her hand, still wary of being this close to her nightmare.

I could have been an evil clown. I could have grabbed her arm and laughed manically "HAHAHA!…

I'VE GOT YOU NOW!!"

I could have guaranteed a child therapist a steady income for years.

Instead, I shook her hand and smiled. I wished her a happy birthday and left.

Fear can be a crippling thing, especially when you are surrounded by clowns all day.

Which ones are evil? Which are good? How can you enjoy the party if your running and hiding all the time?

Even a child can hold out a hand and face fear head on… and sometimes if you do face that fear, you can see the clown for what he is … a clown.

It doesn't mean you still don't have the fear, you just don't let that fear keep you from enjoying the party.

MUSIC AND MEMORIES …

I was going through my old storage unit and came across my 8-track tape collection packed in Naugahyde cases.

I never saw a "Nauga" in my life, but I imagine that they were hunted to extinction for their hides in the Mid-seventies to make couches, beanbag chairs and conversion-van seat covers that would stick to you like superglue if the temperature went above 70 degrees.

As I was looking over these wonderful memories my ten year old niece came over and said, "What are those?"

I felt very old, suddenly …

I explained to her that there was a time…

Long before the MP3 and the Ipod...

Before CDs…

In a time when vinyl records were actually "listened to" on "turntables" and not scratched to pieces as part of rap artists background noise…

In this far away time, shortly after the invention of the wheel and discovery of fire, came the war of "The 8-track" and "The Cassette"…

I wove the tale of superior musical quality… of 8 tracks over the cassettes 4 measly tracks.

The amazing technology of being able to jump instantly at the press of a plastic button to 4 different places on the 8 track at the cheap expense of having one song chopped in half so all the songs would fit on the tape.

It was far superior to "fast forwarding" and "rewinding" a cassette to your favorite songs.

I spoke of how, in that dark time, mankind embraced the inferior cassette and the 8-track went the way of the Dodo bird.

It was a story of an earlier simpler time.

Now I remember looking at those tapes… Jethro Tull, The Moody Blues, Creedence Clearwater Revival, The Grateful Dead, Fleetwood Mac … and remembered the first time I heard those artists and songs.

Music can take you to places you have been before.

Holding those 8-tracks I could feel the music within them and when I first listened to them as a kid

My first record album was the Doors *13*.

My second was the Beatles *Help* album.

I first listened to these albums on a plastic box record player with the speakers that clipped onto the sides when the cover was closed.

I remember upgrading to a console stereo as a teen with 8 track AND cassette built in, and these 8 tracks were played over and over again,

I remember my first pioneer component stereo,

my first boom box,

my first Walkman cassette player,

my first cd player,

and now I have an iPod that has over 10,000 songs in it.

Jethro Tull, The Moody Blues, Creedence Clearwater Revival, The Grateful Dead, Fleetwood Mac.

I still think it's amazing that I can hold in my hand a device no bigger than a single cassette and hold more music than every vinyl album, 45, cassette, 8 track, and reel to reel that I ever owned.

I love music, all types from classical to heavy metal, industrial to folk, Goth rock to bubble pop

We make more music every moment of every day, and each of us listens to more music every day.

We are musical creatures, so music can take you to places you have been before.

It can trigger memories thought forgotten.

It can take you to different times and chapters in your life.

Music has power. It has the ability to even take you to places you have never been before.

Music can inspire you.

It can soothe you.

Music draws us together, it is a common ground.

Music is important.

The Gorilla, The Panda, The Bunny …

Experiences lead to other experiences. The doors we open lead to other doors, sometimes doors we wouldn't have found otherwise,

Send in the clown, part two.

The first time I put on the gorilla suit I was worried that it fit me just a little too well,

It made me wonder if the reason I like bananas might be a little more than just me liking bananas.

Driving down the highway with a trunk full of balloons, hairy arm hanging out the window in the full moon light.

This is an experience that comes from a carefully walked path thru the mild underbrush of what we call a normal world.

I found that if you wear a gorilla suit long enough you even start to feel more primitive, and what I mean by long enough…

was about 2 minutes…

You start wanting to make noises like "Oooo – Ooo – Oooo.

I could almost hear the host of Wild Kingdom giving commentary in the background.

"And here we find the Urban silverback gorilla in his native habitat, driving down the road in an 85 Oldsmobile Caliente. Ooh and watch closely, a car is driving up next him… the people look over toward the gorilla, and yes the gorilla looks over and smiles, startling the elderly couple as they slam on their brakes and head for the ditch!"

Before I got to the party to deliver a trunk full of air, I had to pull over for gas. (The '85 Oldsmobile Caliente was not well known for its gas mileage.)

So now you have to imagine a typical gas station attendant watching a big black gorilla pumping gas at about 8 o'clock at night, then after the ape finishes, comes in and says, "It's a jungle out there, you work and slave all day for what? Bananas." … the gorilla pays for his gas, and leaves.

I have no idea what the gas station attendant was thinking that night, but I'm sure that he still thinks it to this day.

Pandas are cuter than gorillas, and delivering a panda gram is like any other courier job.

You take your message, deliver it to an address and give the recipient the message…

Only in a panda suit.

It can be a letter, a greeting or a package, delivered by a cute and cuddly panda bear.

What made this day's delivery special was that the person gave me an address but did not tell me what business it was.

So you can imagine MY surprise, and the shocked surprise of everyone in the building when I walked into the bank lobby wearing a giant panda suit and carrying a large paper bag.

I had everyone's undivided attention.

My surprise was nothing compared to the look of surprise on the security guards faces as they were quickly

106

deciding if Ling Ling the half-crazed panda bear needed to be put to sleep.

After a quick interrogation and pat down of the giant panda and determining the contents and recipient of the paper bag, good old Ling Ling went on his merry way.

There is a distant memory deep within myself of standing on an ancient Northern shoreline wearing a helmet with fur.

This memory came back to me as my head was inside another fur helmet, only this helmet had pink and white bunny ears and was shaped like a beach ball with giant buck teeth.

Instead of standing on the shoreline I was standing at the door of a kindergarten class, carrying a large basket of colored chicken eggs.

Yeah that's right, I was Peter Freaking Cottontail on steroids…

So I was supposed to come in, deliver the Easter eggs and leave…

But oh no … that's not good enough for the kids hyped up on chocolate Easter eggs…

They want the fat man in the bunny suit to dance …and dance he must, lest a dark shadow forever be cast upon the legend of the Easter bunny…

And who am I to dash the hopes and beliefs of young ones such as these?

So dance I did, and somehow over the course of many centuries I have gone from living as a mighty warrior along the banks of some distant Nordic shore, to doing the bunny hop with a giant white pompom on my butt…

Over and over again and again…

I don't believe in hell, but …

After about 20 minutes of hopping around with fifty pounds of fur in a hot classroom wearing a fully enclosed 15 pound beach ball on my head I was imagining visions of local news crews and images of animal enforcement carrying away the body of what looked like a big white and pink bunny rabbit, children crying and asking, "Why won't the Easter bunny wake up?" A white paw falling off of the hospital cart and an Easter egg slowly falling to the ground, fade to black…

After breathing my own hot air over and over again I suddenly felt that instead of being surrounded by kindergarteners, I was surrounded by some ancient cannibalistic pygmy tribe dancing around me and that hassenpfeffer was on the menu…

I barely escaped with my life.

I am the gorilla…I am the panda… I am the bunny… these are all masks I have worn.

They are part of the experience that is my life and they are a part of me.

All of us wear masks in our lives…

Masks to protect us.

Masks to hide behind.

Masks that may or may not be a part of who we are really.

Sometimes the masks are scary.

Sometimes the masks furry and warm.

Like the gorilla mask, if you wear a mask long enough you will become like the mask you wear.

Like the panda mask, what you see and interpret to be who you are can be seen to be something totally different to someone else.

Like the bunny mask, sometime the mask we wear can suffocate who we really are.

Look at the masks you wear. Wear the masks that reflect who you really are.

Get rid of the masks that suffocate, that keep you breathing your own sweat and fear.

Swap the masks you hide behind for masks that show who you are and who you want to be.

We wear masks and makeup for many reasons…

You might wear clown makeup like spackle to hide the cracks on your face, or the cracks in your life.

You may hide behind a mask to keep from being vulnerable and hurt.

You can still wear makeup, you can still wear masks, but use the makeup to focus and highlight the natural color and features you have in your life. Everyone has them.

When you concentrate on the beauty you don't see the cracks.

Find something you like about yourself and make a mask out of that.

You don't have to show the world everything that you are, but you don't have to hide behind a mask either.

You will become like the masks that you wear.

Make sure you have enough holes in it to breathe. That's important.

It's been many years since I've put on the clown makeup, but I'm still a clown.

I still like bananas, I like coloring eggs, and once in a while I'll throw some extra bamboo shoots on my plate before walking over to the Mongolian grill…

A Definition of Gravity…

"The natural force of attraction between any two massive bodies, which is directly proportional to the product of their masses and inversely proportional to the square of the distance between them."

This is not what was going through my head a while ago when I fell out of the back of my tractor trailer.

Actually the first thing to go through my head was a rather rude expletive.

The second thing to go through my head was that this was going to hurt a lot.

The third thing to go through my head was the cement pavement. Or I should say it tried to go through my head? When I woke up a second later I realized I was a prophet, as my premonition was accurate.

It did hurt. A lot.

I don't like hospitals. They're too clean. Everything is all white and shiny silver and the conditioned filtered air doesn't smell right. It's not natural.

I was reminded of this as I lay propped up in a bed at St. Lukes Hospital in Newburgh, NY.

The doctor came in and asked me how I was doing.

I told her I had a splitting head ache.

I was diagnosed with a concussion and they sent me down for a CAT scan. I thought "Oh good, I like cats…"

There were no cats involved.

But what they do is put you in this giant white and shiny silver donut and proceed to shoot x-rays into your skull. The nurse who was doing the CT scan comforted me by saying, "It's ok, this won't hurt at all," and then went to stand behind a lead lined blast shield.

I don't like hospitals.

I was at the hospital for 5 hours and during that time I thought about gravity.

I started to think about all the things over the years I had dropped on my feet. Everything that has fallen on me from various heights of various weights. All of the times I had tripped.

I slowly came to the conclusion that while gravity does really nice things, like keeping me from being flung off the earth at 900 plus miles an hour and such, it really wasn't my close friend.

So the bad news was indeed I did have a concussion.

The good news is that I have a very thick skull.

Now this is something that people have been telling me for years, but now I actually have x-ray proof.

I spent the month sitting around the house nursing headaches and watching SpongeBob cartoons, which seem to be a whole lot funnier now. That worries me a little.

I know that gravity doesn't hate me, I just know that it took advantage of the situation.

It's important to know where the ground is and to know where you're stepping before you let go. Being aware of what's around you and what you're jumping into can mean all the difference between being safely grounded or having a whole lot of headaches.

Darwinism and Traffic Circles…

I was going around the Kingston, NY traffic circle when a car, without even looking, pulled out in front of my truck off the highway.

In the car was the driver, who since I don't know his name, I shall call Mr. Darwin. Sitting next to him was Mrs. Darwin.

And in the back seat, screaming and shivering for their lives, watching a 64 thousand pound tractor trailer about to crash into them, sat Buffy and Jody, the Darwin children.

This message is for Buffy and Jody.

There is a reason why stupid people in general are very fertile.

It's called Darwinism.

Take a look at the sea turtle. Sea turtles lay hundreds of eggs far up on the shores of a beach, bury them in dirt and then walk away.

There is a reason they lay hundreds of eggs…

Many of them are dug up and eaten by predators before they even hatch.

They are the lucky ones.

Some hatch and dig their way out of the dirt, and start heading down the beach, where many of them are attacked from above and eaten by seagulls. The survivors then make it to the safety of the water, where many of them are eaten by fish or scooped up by pelicans. The remaining few, screaming and shivering for their lives, find shelter and live for another day.

I apologize if the loud sound of my airhorn frightened you. Unfortunately the airhorns on big rigs can't yell out, " What the Hell? Are you insane!!!"

All they can do is go beep, really, REALLY loud.

I'm sure by now that you realize as you were looking at the front of a tractor trailer two feet from your terrified faces, that, indeed, your parents have buried you in the sand, turned their backs and walked away, and that your own survival depends on you.

Your chances of being chewed to death by a pelican have greatly increased.

And finally, if something happens to you, your parents will just make a couple more of you, because THAT is how Darwinism works.

So my brakes held and the Darwin family lived for another day.

I talk about the journey all the time. Our lives are a journey, yet I think people are too caught up in the destinations. It's good to have goals. It's good to know where you want to go in life. We all start where we are and we all end up at another place, but I think people are so concerned about the places they want to go that they forget about all the space in between.

The journey is not about where you stop, it's about all that space. The decisions we make, the sights we see along the way, the things we learn on the path and what we do with it.

Don't look so far ahead to where you are going that you are not looking at what is around you now.

There are traffic circles in life, there are tractor trailers out there. You need to slow down and really look around you. Awareness is the key to the journey.

118

Evolution and the Snow Sled…

We had our first real snow storm of the season the other day and it brought back some memories of my childhood and snow sledding.

While my brain tells me these were fun times and remembers walking up the steep hills in a winter wonderland and the thrill of starting down the hill ,things get a bit fuzzy after that.

Bits and pieces of blocked memory involving trees, pricker bushes and snow.

Lots and lots of snow.

The sleds themselves for me was an evolution.

It started with a cardboard box, broken flat and the top edge pulled back like a toboggan.

The only flaw was that you could feel every pebble on your backside all the way down the hill. Or at least until you hit the small rise about three-quarters of the way down, then you didn't feel anything.

The bump didn't look like much when you walked up the hill but when you hit it at 70 miles per hour, on your butt, you knew it was there.

The trick was that as you were airborne you had to stay attached to you sled.

This is not possible when your sled is a piece of battered cardboard.

It is very peaceful when you're soaring through the air… very quiet.

Bad things happen in that silence.

In the movies, when things are quiet, that's right before the lunatic with an axe jumps out from the cellar stairs.

Or the mama bear protecting her cub comes out from behind a tree and swipes you.

Bad things happen in the silence

The next evolution of my sled involved a device known as a snow saucer.

This was a round dome shaped sled with two handles on it to hold onto, thus solving the problem of sticking to the sled when you hit the bump.

The big flaw with the saucer design was the fact that, being a rather chubby little kid, the saucer basically turned me into a ball with one smooth side…

 and as I went down the hill the ball, namely me, would start to spin.

I would hear this whooshing sound as I went down the hill, until I hit the bump, and then silence.

When things get quiet sometimes the best position to be in is curled up into a ball… Unless you are sailing over your friend's heads like a cannonball heading for the pricker bushes…

Then it's okay to scream, too.

My next sled was what I call the deformed plastic pool sled.

This had a nice flat surface but was shaped like a person so you didn't have the directional spinning problem of the saucer. You started at the top of the hill and laid down in it like it was a shallow coffin. Again the roar of the air rushing by you was nothing compared to the utter silence when you hit that bump quiet is bad.

120

As I already indicated earlier my personal aerodynamic properties are that of a big bumblebee without wings.

Yet the shape of the sled made it possible to glide an incredible distance, slowly angling down until you are driven into the snowbank like a lawn dart.

The flaw in this design being that it acts as a shovel and fills your pants with 150 pounds of snow.

My sled evolution came to its conclusion with one of the oldest and best sleds ever made.

The flexible flyer with steel runners.

The trick with this sled was to melt and rub canning wax onto the runners until you could see your reflection in the steel, and when you laid the sled on packed ice it would start to move under its own weight.

An absolutely incredible machine, and STEERABLE.

So I went down that hill and listened to the rush of the wind in my ears, steered around the bump and marveled at the sound, not of me screaming like a little girl, but of the continued rush of air in my ears. It was an absolute joy as I ran into the trees and bushes at the bottom of the hill.

Yep, lots of memories…

I guess my point is this, in whatever you do physically, emotionally spiritually, listen to the wind in your ears, enjoy the ride, evolve to steer away from the bumps if you can.

But if things in your life suddenly get quiet, that's when you want to be alert and hold on tight. Bad things happen when it gets too quiet.

Polar Bears and Insanity …

A few years ago I went insane for a brief period.

What I mean by that is I was reading the paper and I noticed that the local Boys and Girls Club was having a fundraiser, and being wintertime they thought of having a polar bear dip. This is where insane people for no good reason jump into a frozen pond, only this time they gave you a reason, make money for the Boys and Girls Club.

So I went insane and thought "HEY that sounds like a good idea!"

I went to all my friends and asked, who wants to give money to the Boys and Girls Club. Nothing.

So then I asked, who would pay to see me go jump into a frozen lake? And the money started rolling in.

Sometimes its all in how you ask.

On the day of the event I dragged my insane body over to Snow Pond, just outside of Oakland, Maine. Kind of an ominous name for a pond.

It was a nice warm Maine winter day. About 37 degrees Fahrenheit and the pond had thawed enough that we didn't have to break up too much ice.

There was about 25 to 30 of us insane people who showed up in bathing suits and winter coats.

It was kind of disconcerting to see the fire and rescue team standing nearby. I'm assuming that they just came out for moral support.

I hoped.

How does one prepare to jump in a frozen pond? You don't. You just do it.

So we all stood there and then they blew the whistle, and 30 insane people, like lemmings, started screaming and running for the lake.

(It helps to start screaming before you actually have to.)

When you hit the water it's not bad because it takes quite a while for the messages coming from your feet to reach your brain.

At some point the water reaches a place between the kneecaps and the waist and that's when sanity decides to come back.

And then the screaming stops and shock sets in,

It was like someone dropped a plugged in toaster in the bathtub.

So now you have to picture 30 people twitching and lurching in a frozen pond like a herd of seals who had just watched one of their own pulled under by a great white shark.

Quite hilarious, unless you're one of the twitching lurching seals.

Sanity settled back in and we proceeded to get out of the water about as quick as we got in.

You would think this would help but as was mentioned before, it was only 37 degrees out.

Imagine 30 beautiful ice sculptures of human seals in poses looking like they were running from a great white shark.

It is good to do crazy things now and then for good causes.

The Boys and Girls Club made oodles of money for their programs and I didn't lose any toes to frostbite.

It seemed like it took a few months to fully thaw and now every time I watch nature programs with seals a tear comes to my eye.

I understand now. I understand.

Tapestry …

I want you all to know that one of the ways I see life is as a tapestry,

Every person we meet is woven into our lives, connected forever, and we become part of their tapestry, each person a thread.

Some people we meet for a brief moment in the grocery store, or drive by on the highway, just a stitch here and there.

Others are woven in from beginning to end, there are hidden threads, strings and yarns of different colors and textures.

Each we weave into this picture that we call life.

There are people who you meet in life who you never realize made a difference in your life until later.

Back in high school I was part of the drama class and a theatrical group called Pentangle Players, and throughout high school we performed many different plays and musicals.

So I learned to act, and dance, and sing.

We did a review of Andrew Lloyds Webber's "Cats" where all of us had to dress up like cats.

This worked incredibly well for the ladies, but not so much for the large guy in the middle of the room.

I looked more like a bear than a cat, but we made it work…

I do think it would have been easier if I had been wearing a big sign around my neck that said, I am a cat, not a bear, meow.

Now my biggest fear was getting up in front of people and failing. I really didn't want to freeze up in front of people.

One of the things they tell you to do to help stage fright is picture everyone you see naked.

As a 16 year old in a class full of beautiful women my age it was more of a distraction than a help.

I guess the biggest trick is basically to get out of your own head, stop thinking about possibly messing up.

We would team up with the drama club at our rival school at the other end of town to do dinner theaters. The audience enjoyed a good supper and two short plays. I remember one dinner theater where we did two plays, one was a short murder mystery and the other was a murder comedy. The set prop that tied the two together was an old wooden coffin. For the first play I played the part of the corpse, standing upright, in a coffin. You would think that this would be an easy part.

It's not.

The story line was, that after about ten minutes the rest of the cast would "discover" the dead body.

Namely me.

Standing in a closed coffin for ten minutes while still very much alive can really mess with your head in ways you cannot possibly imagine…

…just the thrill of having that lid opened I think created a desire to reaffirm life… so during rehearsal every time they would open the casket. I would take a deep breath burst out laughing.

The next part was then having to stand there for 20 minutes with my eyes closed not moving not coughing , nothing, and telling myself not to sneeze not to move, not to do anything.

To do that I had to really get out of my own head and be in the moment, not thinking about the myriad ways of failing but just doing.

Sometimes we would miss` line, sometimes we would not be in the right place, and we would practice.

When it came down to showtime, I was in the coffin and I took a deep breath, and told myself to just get out of my own way.

I had a part to play and this is what I had to do, and it went off without a hitch.

The second play I played the part of an Irish cop and right from the beginning I messed up a line. I quickly corrected it and my cast mate and I adlibbed lines to get back to where we were supposed to be.

The audience didn't even know anything had gone wrong.

I heard a comedian once say, if you are born into this world you are given free tickets to the freak show.

If you're born in the United States, you have front row seats.

And I thought about that and thought about all the different actors in this performance called Life. You have the set designers, people who work behind the scenes, you have the actors on stage performing, the musicians in the pit, and you have the audience, and they are part of the act too. Each of us are in the theater and are a grand part of the performance.

Some of us sit in the audience and enjoy the show, some of us are on stage performing. Some are working hard behind the scenes to make the show happen. Sometimes the actors sit down and people from the audience come up to the stage.

This is life.

We are all freaks in the freak show and we all have a part to play, and I think about how scary it can be to perform. This is where you need to get out of your head, to get out of our own way and just be.

It's good to make plans and prepare, but people will forget their parts. Lines will get screwed up and people will not be in their proper places.

And there will be a lot of adlibbing going on.

Yet the bottom line in Life is be in the moment…

Have fun…

It's showtime …

About the Author

Born in 1965 in Southern New England, Robert, as "Greywolf Moonsong" has been the host of "A Pagan Heart in Maine Podcast" since 2007. When he is not writing and recording you can find him in his art studio painting.

Robert lives in Southern Maine with his wonderful wife Sandy, their roommate Alta and their cat Salem.